Wh...
Stories from the Chicago StreetWise Community

by Anthony Mateos

Published 2025 by Books On A Whim.
Chicago

ISBN: 9-781300-510086

Copyright © 2025 by Anthony Mateos.
All rights reserved.

booksonawhim@gmail.com

Cover art by Vinegarice Design.

StreetWise Magazine

StreetWise magazine is an award-winning weekly publication that features stories about homelessness, poverty, injustice, inequality, and life in Chicago.

Magazine Vendors

Selling StreetWise magazine provides a flexible employment opportunity. It is a job. The vendors buy the magazine for $1.15. They sell it for $3.00, and they keep $1.85 plus tips.

StreetWise vendors are self-employed micro-entrepreneurs. They build relationships and create connections between and across communities that change perceptions about homeless and low-income individuals.

StreetWise Community

StreetWise is a community that honors the dignity of each individual. In March 2020 StreetWise became part of YWCA Metropolitan Chicago's portfolio of comprehensive human services.

www.streetwise.org

Introduction

I was first introduced to StreetWise in 2019 when my mom and I visited their office in the Uptown neighborhood of Chicago. My mom was recording a video at StreetWise for her work at National Louis University. I was 11, so I don't recall all the details, but I vividly remember the vendors I interacted with, the office surroundings, and most notably, the mission of StreetWise.

"StreetWise exists to elevate marginalized voices and provide opportunities for individuals to earn an income with dignity. Anyone who wants to work has the opportunity to move themselves out of crisis."

I wasn't aware of it back then, but StreetWise had been in my life before this visit. When I was a young child there was a magazine vendor near my house who was consistently full of life, and I listened to his lively stories about Evanston, which is my hometown. This StreetWise vendor was a staple in my neighborhood, and at the StreetWise office, I met many more vendors like him. These occasions sparked my idea to create this book.

Like StreetWise's mission, I wanted to help lift up the vendors' voices. Through this book, I hope to embody their mission as best as possible. I set out for this book to reach three main goals to get across to the readers.

- Gain a greater understanding of what StreetWise is.
- Discover the stories of the StreetWise vendors.
- Find out how to support people facing homelessness in Chicago.

This book supports StreetWise by spreading awareness of its mission and sharing the narratives of vendors. In line with my third goal, I decided that all sales generated from this book will go to the StreetWise organization.

Before thinking up this book, I wanted to contribute to building a better community by presenting inspirational tales of people overcoming obstacles. It took me a couple of years to figure out the topic for my project. Ultimately, I chose to focus on StreetWise due to my admiration for their mission.

Writing this book began with my contacting the StreetWise staff to confirm their agreement with my project. After that, my main task was interviewing the vendors one-on-one at the StreetWise office, now located on the Near South Side. Most of the interviews took place in the summer of 2024 when I was 16.

I audio-recorded and transcribed the interviews and pieced together the most meaningful parts, capturing vendors' personal experiences that relate to the organization.

All StreetWise vendors participated voluntarily to support this book. I also interviewed StreetWise supporters and staff members. I am extremely thankful to everyone I interviewed. Without these conversations, this project would not have been possible.

The vendors I had the good fortune to talk with are some of the bravest people I have ever encountered. They shared their vulnerabilities with me when they talked about their struggles, and this takes bravery. A common thread across all of the conversations was their sense of pride and increased self-esteem through their entrepreneurial work selling the magazine.

The vendors' stories moved me immensely. The hardships that many vendors have faced are incredibly important to understand. Their stories expand our insight into their situations. This is also why reading StreetWise magazine is so valuable. StreetWise magazine, as you will learn, amplifies the voices of Chicago communities.

Every supporter and staff member I spoke with shares the same goal of creating a means for challenged individuals to have a job that grants them independence and a livable income.

StreetWise is not a charity but an opportunity for employment for those who need it. Anyone who walks through the doors of the StreetWise office has the opportunity to become a magazine vendor and begin working for themselves. The company has improved the lives of so many people. All of this I find nothing less than extraordinary.

This book is carried on the shoulders of the assistance I have received from the StreetWise supporters, staff, and vendors alike. And also, my mom, who is my role model. Without my mom, this project would not have happened. Throughout every step of the journey, she mentored me in making this project the best version it can be. When I was nine, I joined her in Milwaukee at the Sojourner Truth Center while she interviewed people for her oral history book. My mom's hard work inspired me to follow in her footsteps and create my own oral history book that helps those in need.

Lastly, the main takeaway that I want readers to gain after reading this book is the importance of lifting each other up as a community. In a time when America is significantly divided, it is essential to embrace the value of unity. Strength as a community far outweighs the power a single individual can ever reach. Looking at people eye-to-eye without judgment unites and emboldens us without hate.

I wish to express that my heart goes out to all people—across all communities and populations—who are facing homelessness.

My main hope for you as the reader is to go beyond the pages. Next time you see a vendor selling StreetWise, buy a magazine and talk with them. If you cannot buy a magazine, offer them a smile or a wave. The kindness matters.

Anthony Mateos
March 2025

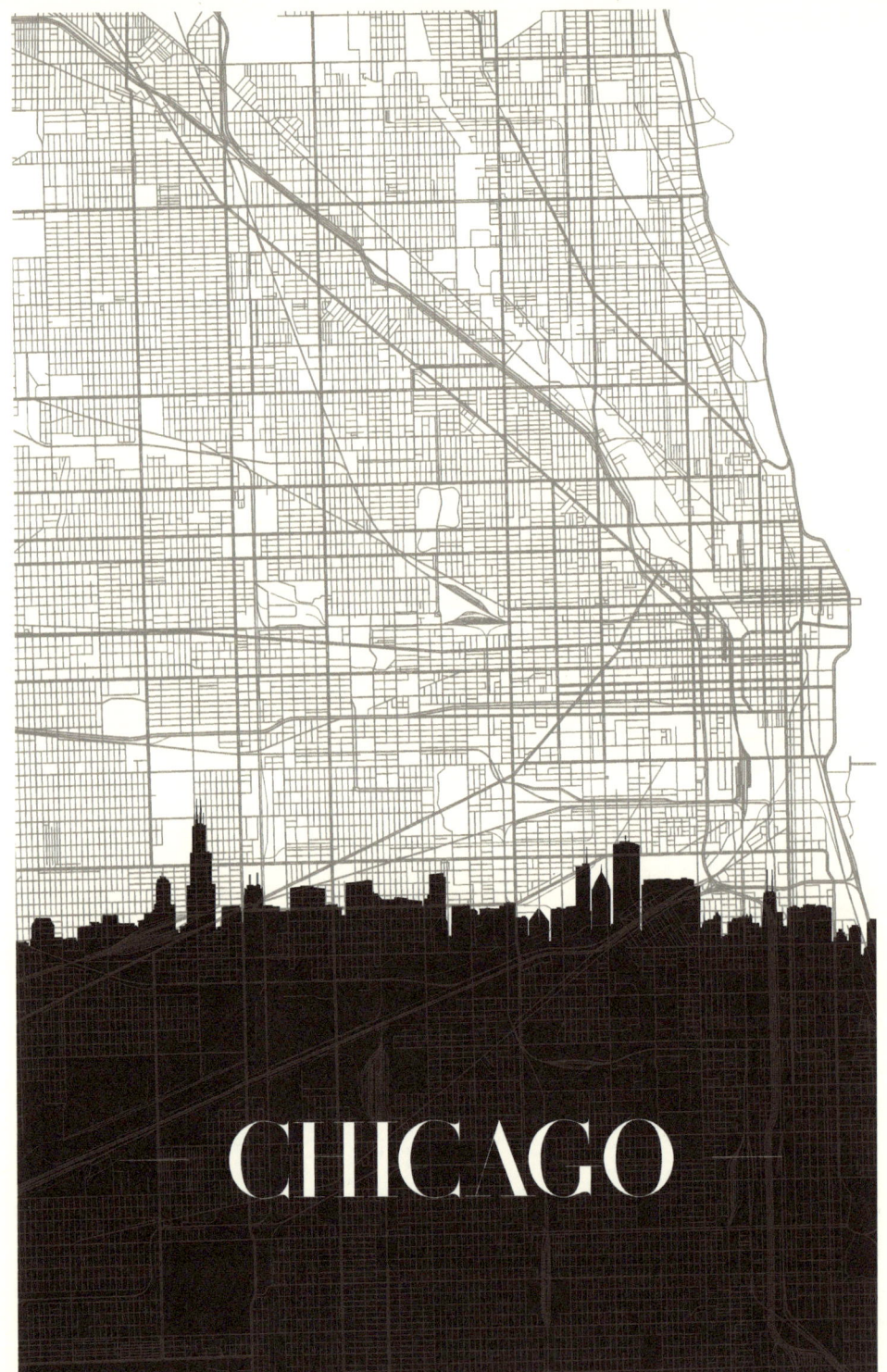

Table of Contents

Freedom – Jimmie 6

Encouragement – Keith 9

Fond Memories – Jacqualine 14

Respect and Dignity – Arturo 15

The Greatest Gift – Cora 17

A Better Picture – Suzanne 21

Everyone Needs Love – Pete 26

The Sense of Hope – Lonnie 30

Wonderfully Supportive – Saul 33

A Greater Empathy – Julie 37

A Communal Experience – A. Allen 40

Proof – Daniel 43

A Blessing – Ruben 45

A Platform for People – Dave 47

Read Up on It – Quanna 51

A Different Kind of World – John 53

Higher Powers – Dre 56

Thankful – Russell 59

Compassionate Hearts – MJ 62

Poem – Roarke 66

Freedom

Jimmie
Vendor

I learned about StreetWise through a friend of mine named Troy who was working for StreetWise. He asked me, "Man, you want to make some real money? Take this number down." He gave me a flyer and put his name on it.

I came down and did the orientation. I got in and got my first 15 magazines for free. I started from there, and I boosted myself from 15 to, like, 70 a week. My first spot was on 53rd and Harper at a Starbucks.

I was out there for, oh, about six years. Then they closed the Starbucks down, and I went to another Starbucks. Loomis and Taylor. I stayed there for maybe five, six years. Things basically didn't work out for me. So, I went to Starbucks on Damen and Irving Park, and that's where I'm at now.

When I'm there, I help keep the place cleaned up. I help the customers if they need anything. I'm there to assist, and they like that about me.

This is a job for me. It's good money, and you get to know people. It builds you up to keep you going. A lot of people love StreetWise. They love the magazine. Sometimes StreetWise puts out editions that go for two weeks. I have the type of clientele that want a new magazine every week.

The will in good people is what inspires me to keep going.

I've been with StreetWise maybe 17 years, and it has helped me and my family out greatly. Since I've been with StreetWise, I've gotten married. I have a son that's in college. My customers support me 100%.

Anything else good that I can say about StreetWise is *everything*. StreetWise staff, editors, and directors are on my side. They have treated me very well since I've been with them. Any complaints that I have, I speak to one of the staff members. They look into it and take care of it.

The StreetWise community is like Spider-Man. Different vendors go about doing things in different ways. They have their own approach with their customers. Vendors have different attitudes. But as far as I know, the StreetWise community is great. It's like your friendly neighborhood Spider-Man. Your friendly neighborhood StreetWise vendor! You're a friendly guy, and you look out for your neighborhood.

Early wake up in the morning, man. Early getting on the spot. Early meeting and greeting my customers, wishing them a good day. That's what I enjoy most. It's freedom, being your own boss. You're doing your own thing, making yourself happy as well as making your customers happy.

Keep a smile on your face. You got to have that smile. Without that smile, no good thing comes. I put the smile on my face. I speak nicely and wisely. "Good morning, how you doing? Have a good day."

But sometimes there are things you have to ignore. Like prejudice. The prejudiced ones won't speak to you. They get their coffee, and on their way out, they'll look at you real cross-eyed and funny-faced, like, "Get out of my face, Black man." You know what I'm saying? Those are the things that you have to ignore.

Once I was at 53rd and Harper when I was selling. I ran into this white police officer. I didn't know he was a police officer.

I asked him, "How would you like a magazine this morning?"

He said, "I don't want no magazine now or ever. Don't you ever ask me if I want a magazine."

So, I'm like, "Sir, I was just asking if you wanted a magazine. You didn't have to get smart with me."

And he didn't show me a badge or anything; he just showed me a gun. So, I went out, and I called the police.

The police came and said, "You know the guy is a police officer."

Well, I'm like, "I didn't see a badge."

Quite naturally, if I don't see a badge, I'm going to call the police. So, I had to go somewhere else for about three weeks and try to sell my magazine. To take a cool off. That was a very bad experience. That's prejudice. But other than that, I haven't had any problems.

Oh, I love everybody here at StreetWise. I have no issues with anyone. Ron is a great guy. Julie is a great lady. Amanda is wonderful. When my father passed, they helped me with my father's funeral. My mother passed, and they helped me with that. When I got my first apartment, they helped me with that. They helped me greatly when I was in need. They were there for me. So, there's nothing bad I can say about StreetWise.

StreetWise picked me up when I was a mess. Once I got with StreetWise, it changed my life. It put hope in front of me.

And the vendors, I get along with them all. They like me, I like them. We're one tag team. It's a joke thing. We point at each other, crack jokes at one another and just have fun.

Chicago is all right. I want to leave Chicago, but Chicago is nice as long as you mind your business. I'm up in age. I'm 68 years old. I like to bowl. I like to play ball with my son. I have a dog I run around and play with.

I'm basically a quiet person.

Encouragement

Keith
Vendor

I learned about StreetWise over 20 years ago. I was homeless and by myself out here in the streets. I happened to see someone selling a newspaper hollering "StreetWise!" So, I went to 13th and Michigan; that's where StreetWise was then. At the time, the orientation was three days long.

Once I learned about StreetWise, things started to change for me. One day I woke up and had money in my pocket. I stopped using drugs and started putting more of myself into my job. Keeping up on my hygiene, my clothing, and my health.

The main motivation for me was making money and being able to do for myself. Oh, it felt so good going to the store and being able to pay for things. After that, I haven't looked back. The whole organization has been good to me.

They helped me out when I needed it. As long as I have my magazines, I have money. It feels good earning my own money—earning it, not begging. I got a product that's informative and lets people know what's going on in the neighborhood.

In 2020, we were at the beginning of the pandemic, and it had the stay-at-home effect. Well, I didn't know how that was going to work out because if I didn't work StreetWise, I didn't eat. I couldn't pay my bills. For a year I was in a hotel spending about $1,050 to $1,085 a month for rent, $35 a day.

When I was working, I thought, "Wow, I can get my own place." But that didn't work out because of my background. Someone from the county, though, allowed me to rent a room. $350, $400 a month. That's a lot better than a thousand eighty-five. So that's where I've been living for the past three or four years.

I got a roof. I feed myself. I clothe myself. I can come here to the StreetWise office. They have little care packages for personal hygiene, clothing, and any help that you could need. One time we had banks of computers. Some vendors are not computer literate. Fortunately, I am. StreetWise staff help you with that. Also, reading. We have people slow at reading sometimes with mental problems. StreetWise does its best to accommodate everyone.

Oh, I've been a vendor over 20 years, off and on. I've become my own boss. I work five days a week, I do four hours a day.

The StreetWise community is a family. We all try to encourage each other. They used to have a team called QAT (Quality Assurance Team), and they go around checking on vendors, seeing if they doing things the proper way. I've this badge, as you see, and you can only sell StreetWise with this badge. You can't sell candy, cigarettes, or nothing else. All you can do is sell StreetWise.

Using the proper language is the proper way. You can't have vendors out there cussing people out because people won't buy the magazine. I let the new vendors know: you miss one customer, you catch another. It's like a bus or a train. Miss one, there'll be another one coming past. Everything takes time and patience.

I get a chance to learn about people. Facial expressions, body language, generosity, un-generosity. I've become a pretty good judge of people's character. People are making these types of facial expressions when they walk past you. They're looking up at the building to not look at you. It's okay. I don't get upset; I just smile and keep it going, keep it moving.

A lot of times the people come back—sometimes hours, sometimes days, sometimes months later. They come back and say, "I've never done this before, but you've been persistent, and I enjoy seeing that smile every day." They buy the magazine and give donations. I enjoy this. I enjoy earning my own money.

That's not to say I don't have challenges. Credit score for one. Being able to use StreetWise as a means of working for my credit score.

People figure StreetWise is just for the homeless, and it's not. StreetWise is for anyone who needs a little help, and now and then everybody does. Birthdays. Holidays.

I'm in the downtown area. I'm on Michigan and Lake Street from 6 a.m. to 10 a.m. As you see, I'm here (in the StreetWise office) now. So, my day is done. I have to take care of other important businesses, like making doctor appointments. I'll be 63 in October. I may look good, but I'm falling apart.

I'm 62. Am I very young? No. Old age, old injuries—shoulder injuries from when I played football. High blood pressure, and things of that nature. A lot of people assume that I'm in good health, but I'm not. I'm constantly seeing doctors and therapists at least three to four times a month. Now what employer will want to hire someone that every other week has got to go to the doctor? Eye doctor on Monday. Teeth on Tuesday. So on, and on, and on.

I like having my own time and putting in the work. A lot of my customers get worried about me. If they don't see me for a day or two, they'll call up to the office and ask, "Hey, where's the vendor on Michigan and Lake? His name is Keith."

StreetWise has encouraged me that I am not alone. This encouragement helps get me up. At 3 o'clock in the morning, I'm up. Every day. At 4:15, I'm out the door. I come down here (to the office), get my cup of coffee, and I put forth the effort with the magazines, and the people seem to enjoy it. Holidays are the best. Oh yeah, Christmas is good.

There's a guy on the street. He's a drug addict. I have to compete with his addiction because he has a cat with him. So, I'm double-competing because people walk past me, up to him, and say, "Here, this is for you and the cat."

They give him $60, $80 at one time. You know, I gotta look at these people. They look past me every day but see him. They wouldn't buy a three-dollar magazine from me. "Well, that's for him and the cat," they say. You know damn well that cat ain't gonna see no money. This man's using that cat as a crutch to get money. Even Black folks will go to him before they will me. It teaches me about the different attitudes of different people and the way they see things.

I just shake my head, smile about it, and thank the Lord for another day of showing me the right way. I take care of myself. I don't impose on no one. My customers enjoy seeing my smile and hearing my laughter in the morning. I joke around with them.

I have a lot of friends here at StreetWise. We used to have picnics over at Lincoln Park and barbecues during the summer. The staff talk to you if you have a problem.

Well, I've had problems. I've had dirt thrown in my face. I've been called a (n-word) in the middle of Michigan and Lake Street over and over. I've been spit on, and that's just between last year and this year. The staff, I let them know.

I thank God every morning I open my eyes. Because it ain't promising. What little health that I do have, I thank Him for.

The vendors that I've met have their own ways of doing and selling. Some people move around; I don't. I've established me a corner. They ought to name it after me when I leave.

Like I said, I've got health issues and appointments. I'm trying to get my social security disability. I've been denied twice before over the years. This time around I have a lawyer who's gonna represent me. I've been told by Social Security that my education was too expensive to warrant me being on disability. They tell me that I should be able to get a job if I ain't got to lift over 10 pounds. But they forget about my background. They're not paying attention.

You know, I believe in the Lord God, and I thank Him for every day, and I praise Him. My spirit is with everyone.

My attitude towards life is a lot different than what it was before StreetWise. I had just given up. My mom died from breast cancer. My pop, he passed away from heart problems and colon cancer. Oh man, it was tremendous on me. When you think your burden is too much to handle, let go to God. I put it in His hand, and He's always come up with a way to say, "Hey, I got you." By the end of the day, I find myself saying, "Man, okay, I could do this." It turns out pretty well.

I did some modeling. I've had articles written about me inside the magazine. We've had a few galas. I've been there and rubbed elbows with some of the bigwigs that were congressmen and aldermen.

Where I'm at on Michigan and Lake, I've met a few celebrities. Frazier, Rod Stewart. They're walking by.

"Hey, Frazier. Hey, Rod. How you doing?" Wow.

And he's like, "I'm not Rod."

And I said, "Yeah, you is."

"No, I'm not."

I said, "Look at your shoes." He got gym shoes on with the British flag on it.

He got to smiling and shook his head, and he said, "How did you know?"

I said, "You look like yourself. I've been listening to your music since I was a kid."

He's like, "Well, shh, don't tell nobody."

"Oh, your secret safe with me."

When I used to sell on the Gold Coast, down there on Rush Street, there was a famous ex-cop named Steve Wilkos with Jerry Springer. I sold Jerry Springer a magazine or two. Now, some other vendors get to meet with baseball and hockey celebrities.

I had a little skit in a commercial promoting how Chicago works. They played it before every Blackhawks game. A lot of my customers that enjoy hockey come and say, "I saw you on the jumbo board at the United Center. Great job!"

Well, since the pandemic, things have slowed down tremendously. Now it's hard for me to even sell 30 magazines in a week. I used to do 30 magazines a day.

I would like to continue doing what I'm doing. I hope that things pick up and I'll be able to get my own place. That I ain't got to rent from no one else. I can get subsidized housing.

Yeah, that's the goal for me right now. Once you get old, you'll be like, "Ah, forget about it." But that's about it.

Fond Memories

Jacqualine
Vendor

I was born in 1961. Born and raised in Chicago. I lived in Englewood. A long time ago there was a lady that was handing out flyers, and she was telling me about StreetWise. I waited a long time to come to StreetWise. I came in 2011. I wanted to make a little extra money on the side. Just wanted some extra money to spend.

I sell it on Wacker Drive by the Opera House. Oh, I've been invited out to plays, to operas. Customers give you food sometimes. They give you lots of food. One time a man gave me a backpack full of money. It was a backpack with food and like $60. It was a nice backpack.

StreetWise helps you reach your goals. You set goals for yourself, and you reach them. I enjoy meeting people. I get to enjoy different things I wouldn't normally experience if I wasn't a vendor.

I made a ton of friends. I've been to a lot of StreetWise parties and lunches. A lot of fond memories. The StreetWise staff, we have a good relationship. They help you get on your feet.

I have enough money to meet my basic needs. Like, say, for instance, bills. They give you clothes, they give you food, toiletries, stuff like that.

My hobbies include knitting, watching movies, and being with friends. Selling StreetWise is a challenge, but it's a good challenge. People are mostly friendly. My passion is to keep being a streetwise person. I'm a streetwise person.

Respect and Dignity

Arturo
Vendor

I have been a StreetWise vendor for the last 20 years. The corner of LaSalle and Monroe is my usual spot for selling my newspapers from the very early hours of every morning.

I am so grateful for my customers who are very kind and generous with me. A few months ago, my heart was filled with much pain and sorrow, as I found my companion during these early hours of the day dead just a few feet away. Pinto lay on the sidewalk with a broken wing. My companion, who was a multi-colored pigeon, had been with me at that corner for many years during our Chicago hot summer days and the freezing winter ones.

I became homeless over 20 years ago as I walked in the West Side of our city during the early morning hours going to my full-time work as a machine operator. Two gang members attacked me, and after stealing twenty dollars from me, shot two bullets into my head for no reason known to me.

I was taken to the nearby hospital where I remained for a number of weeks. Highly dedicated and caring doctors and nurses saved my life. But, unfortunately, the two bullets had done much brain damage. My right arm remains paralyzed to this day, and my left leg often drags behind me when I walk.

I did know some English 20 years ago. However, after the gunshots, I can only speak my native Spanish very slowly and at times with some difficulty. And I make sure I take my daily medication to avoid seizures.

When I saw my companion pigeon with his broken wing a few months ago, my eyes filled with tears. He had been very faithful to me over the years. And now he was gone. After leaving the hospital 20 years ago, I was taken to a respite program on the West Side of our city for people who are homeless and still recovering after leaving area hospitals. It was a wonderful place to recover and relearn to walk again without a walker. The staff and other residents treated me with much respect and dignity. And the healthcare staff also continued to support me in the healing that was ongoing.

However, after a number of months at the respite center, I left on my own. There was no housing available for the majority of the program's residents who were ready to move on. So, for the next 12 years, I survived sleeping in the streets, and at times in the shelters of our city.

I also sold StreetWise. I was grateful that I had some money for food and moving around the city. And then one day nine years ago, as I sold my StreetWise magazine at Monroe and LaSalle and accompanied by my friend Pinto, a social worker approached me. A few weeks later I was able to move into my own apartment, which is part of the Samaritan Program, run by the Center for Housing and Health and H.O.W., Inc.

My heart filled with gratitude as I was able to make my own bed after 11 years of homelessness, even with only one arm. I have been there ever since, but always faithful to my customers at Monroe and LaSalle every morning. And in the mornings, I am now accompanied by my new pigeon friend, Pinto II, whom I believe is the daughter of my dead companion.

Written with the support of my friend, Mr. A. Bendixen.

The Greatest Gift

Cora
Vendor

I'm Cora. I first learned about StreetWise when I was going through a rough period in my life, as far as financial. I have always been one to donate to causes, whether it's StreetWise, Easterseals, or whoever.

To be honest with you, something was missing in my life. I wanted to be able to reach a broader range of people. I'd been praying on it. So, when the opportunity did come up, it was pivoting.

I was going up to the store, Mariano's, and I ran into a guy named Allen. He was selling StreetWise for $3. I used to always give money and then keep going. But this time I wanted to know exactly what StreetWise was about. Now I've been a vendor for a little over two years.

I'm a lover of people. I can talk to anybody no matter what country they're from. I wanted to be able to get out and tell my story. I wanted to share the willingness that anything is possible. You have to want it. I can't want it for you more than you. StreetWise gives you tools to work to better your life, but it's really up to you to do the betterment. Make sense?

I have run into people that have been big supporters of StreetWise for years and years and years. You have to get out there and, for lack of a better word, be in the trenches with people. Some people were just like me: people that were lost, people that were hurting.

You may see people on the corner with a jar in their hand. And you're quick to judge these particular people. I do myself. However, you don't know what people's situation is and background. I say to myself, "By the grace of God, there go I. Was not I at one point there?"

Vendors work in different places. Some people tend to go wherever they choose, like myself, where I'm not boxed in. I recognize the vendors, I respect them. I respect their boundaries, as far as if they're selling papers there.

I don't have no challenges. I'm streetwise and street-smart. If someone cusses me out on the street, that's not a challenge. That's people deflecting. That's how they feel. I'm going to honor how they feel because that's not who I am.

Sometimes, I may be offered sex. I may be offered drugs. I may be offered alcohol. All I said was, "Would you like to contribute to StreetWise? We've been out here 32 years, empowering people to help people get their lives together." Or I find myself saying something like, "I really don't appreciate you offering me weed." I've always been taught to keep my side of the street clean.

I sell StreetWise in Rogers Park, Edgewater, Andersonville, the Gold Coast, Millennium Park, and the South Side of Chicago. Wherever I go, I can sell my magazines. I'm talking to people because I like people's perspectives. I like learning about cultures. People are coming over here from Ukraine and Russia. I say, "Tell me something about your country that's different from ours." I love learning. So, that's what I find exciting about working for StreetWise. For me it's the people, it's not the monetary.

I don't want to only think for myself. With just my little bitty thinking I would know so little. For me, it is hearing others' ideas and learning about other people. I was talking to somebody out in Rogers Park and... where was she from? Ethiopia, I think. She knew my name. Wherever I go, they remember my name. I say, "Thank you so much for the donation. Enjoy your day."

You get to embrace other people that genuinely care about people. I speak to the students at Columbia College, at Northwestern, and Loyola. I tell them the importance of being vigilant about their surroundings, or if they're visiting, I'm like, "Hey, if you go out and have a drink, if you go to the bathroom, when you come back, don't drink that drink."

Hey, Chicago is a beautiful place. However, Chicago has its potholes. When people are looking for people to rob, they look for people who's not aware. If you're looking at the phone, you're not paying attention. If you happen to be unaware and someone walks up to you with a gun, give them whatever they want. You can't get your life back. It's not worth it. The phone, whatever. If it was me, I'd say, "Hey, wait a minute, do you want the shoes too?"

It's more important to value yourself over materialistic things. Also, I'm self-conscious about what I put in my body. I'm wise enough to know that health is wealth.

One of the biggest things StreetWise has given me is the freedom. I've been in institutions all my life. I cannot be boxed in. I asked myself this question, "Did the system fail me or did I fail the system?" So, I'm out wanting to redirect people. To let people know that no matter what you've been through in life, you have a choice. I tell them, "Your story can make a difference in somebody's life." I want to give people hope.

At 69 years young, if I'm not feeling well, I can call the office and let the staff know. Or sometimes I'm taking a class, doing some things over at Goodman Theatre. I'm very vocal about the different things that I'm doing. I may call in if I'm doing service work at Care for Real, volunteering. Yes, I do StreetWise, but it's more than that.

I am actually going now to the Daley Plaza because they have shows at 12 o'clock for Children Matter. I go to engage and embrace.

StreetWise gave me a bigger vision. If I'm hungry, they'll feed me. They have the coffee here for people. They have a clothing closet. I'm out there letting people know that they can also donate clothes. They don't have to have the tag on it. It's a hand up and not a hand down.

I've had quite a few interesting customers. A few newscasters. I ran into Pat Quinn, who used to be our governor, at an event StreetWise did on Michigan Avenue. He knew me personally. I've been incarcerated, and I'm one of them people that when you talk to me, you're not going to forget me. Because I'm down to earth. People respect integrity and when you be honest.

I was locked up when I was about nine years old. A mental institution to jails, all these homes, just locked up. This was all due to addiction. We're talking about nine years old and being put in a system and being told that you had a nervous breakdown because your dad died. Giving you medication. Strapping a kid down and shooting him up with Thorazine.

Some of the experiences is what make me who I am today. I'm very resilient. I'm a warrior. I have no excuses. I take accountability. Yes, I did make mistakes. Yes, I took from people. Yes, I did burglary thefts. Because drugs don't care about that.

Drugs say "Come get me at all costs." I'm just grateful I ain't never tried to kill nobody to get drugs. Just was always trying to get the drug, and once I got the drug, it didn't matter how much money I had. I would always give a lot of it away to people less fortunate than me. Because, see, I'm out there in the trenches with them, and I understand what a lot of people's struggles are.

Did I feel good about taking from others? No, but when you're in addiction you're not thinking about that. It's only when you've been sober, now almost five years, when your mind begins to sober up. You get a chance, that quiet time. You stay by yourself and reflect on your life. You're wise enough to know that you have more time behind you than in front of you.

When people ask me, so what is the greatest gift you can give to anyone? A lot of people think it's love. I think the greatest gift you can give to anyone is forgiveness. It's so hard for people to forgive themselves and forgive others.

A Better Picture

Suzanne
Editor-in-Chief

I'm Suzanne Hanney, and I am a native Chicagoan, and my goal is to show Chicago stories.

We put out a publication that the vendors can sell, and it talks about better ways for Chicago to help people who are marginalized live better. In other words, how do we all live a good life in Chicago? How do we equalize as much as possible, because that is what America is about?

I'm very into the city. The city is a kind of gritty place. It's where a lot of people come to make money because there's this energy, and there are opportunities. There's this cross of people.

By nature, the city is a crazy place with so much going on that stuff may fall by the wayside, and that's okay. People are meeting and becoming creative and feeding off of each other's ideas. So, I'm all about "How do we encourage that?" Because that's how people make contacts, find jobs, or find ways to create businesses that improve their lives.

I grew up in Chicago, and I went to journalism school at Medill. Politics was my second nature. Why? Well, because it was germane to what I wanted to do. I am the granddaughter of immigrants. My father died when I was nine. My mother raised me as a single mom, widowed. So, I'm not that far removed from the people I cover.

Chicago is getting to be more and more elite. When that happens, there's less and less middle class, which means that it's more difficult for low-income people to make it. That's happening in the country as a whole because of wealth transfers. When one generation dies, they hand over their wealth to the next generation. It's a snowball effect because whites have traditionally had larger estates than Blacks have, or their housing has been worth more, so when they pass it on, it snowballs. This is what is known as the racial wealth gap.

It takes money to make money, and people don't understand that. We tend to worship heroes, and we expect people to overcome difficult circumstances, but not everyone is that strong. Some people just want to live good, basic lives, and they can still be newsworthy. People can't start from nothing and make it in this economy. I try to draw those parallels in my stories.

I'm usually doing the hard work of writing. I will look at emails to see if there's a press release that I will throw into what's called my "From the Streets" file. I intend to do short bits of news that are related to big news. I found a short press release about an ordinance on the Northwest Side. It's a proposed ordinance that would impose a demolition fee on multi-family homes that go into single-family homes. A group is proposing that as a way to keep affordable housing. So that's a short story I can do.

I found another story about scholarships being awarded to minority kids. It was partly with the Urban League and partly with a law firm. I thought that was a neat story because when I was growing up, newspapers were almost like Facebook. They were much more about the community and the neighborhood. They weren't just about the hard, hard news, but rather news about people doing little things.

Newspapers gave you a better picture of what the overall society was like. I want StreetWise to be that way too. I want readers to have the same excitement I have as a reporter—finding short stories that tell you about the ways the city runs. You just stay fluid on your feet.

Vendors will talk about the neighborhoods that they know and like. So, I suggest spots for the vendors. John and A. Allen (Field Supervisors) have ideas as well. I've seen various reader studies over the years, and they pretty much all say the same thing. The StreetWise reader is highly educated, highly paid and has influential jobs. So, vendors go where those people are. That's marketing. Those people are going to frequent Starbucks and bookstores. They care about things like social justice, education, and the environment. Traditionally, they're mostly women. So, you know that vendors should be in places where women would shop.

Pretty much it's me and it's Dave (Creative Director) writing the stories, and then I have a few freelancers. I have other volunteer writers, and I'm trying to do more of that because I want to get more grassroots views. In addition to grassroots views, I want to get more decision-maker views. I want readers to be able to see in a simple way what power people have to say about how things move.

We did the Chicago Neighborhood Development Awards, which is the Oscars of neighborhood development. Toni Preckwinkle, who's the County Board President, talked about one award winner, Marilyn Katz, who has died. Marilyn got the award posthumously for "Friend of the Neighborhood." Marilyn was a public relations person who suggested that Mayor Johnson meet with the Cardinal because there are lots of churches that are empty, and they could use them for migrant housing.

That was a unique story because she said something that personal, and it's about how the city runs. I also want more stories where individual people on the street can say, "This is how I wish Chicago would run."

I'm doing a lot of stories about women who had interesting lives, but I'm picking that up from their obituaries. Now, why is it the obituaries are the only thing that remains that give us that very familiar kind of news?

Like, one woman was a champion Irish fiddler, and another set of women started an agency that delivered infant formula to shelters when the Women, Infants, and Children's program had cutbacks. And another woman started a nursing curriculum.

I also want StreetWise to be fun and breezy. I don't want to say we tend to write the bad news, because that's not true. Life is actually good, and news is...new. I like to say news is the plural of new. Bad things are news because they are out of the ordinary—new. But we tend to see so much bad all the time that we don't realize that news can be good.

Vendors come up with ideas too. One vendor asked me if we could do an edition on Tina Turner. I asked, "What's the relevance to StreetWise?" Then another vendor, A. Allen, the other Field Supervisor, said that he had met Tina Turner when he was a child, and he wanted to do a column on her.

At that point, I had two reasons for doing the Tina Turner issue. I researched her life and found more reasons. Tina Turner was a domestic violence victim, and I don't know if most people realize that. She had to escape with literally nothing. Then she opened for a lot of rockers. She networked with all these people, and they helped her. That's how she came back.

That's how you get out of homelessness, too. You have to have friends. I tell people that the real reason people are homeless is isolation. They don't have anybody to give them contacts, a job, or a place to stay.

Another reason for doing the issue was that Tina Turner had kidney disease, which also affects Black people more. Kidney disease only really affects 1% of the population, but it's 6% of the Medicaid budget. If you have kidney disease, you might need more dialysis, more treatment. You may ultimately need a new kidney.

Kidney disease links to blood pressure. One of the ways to avoid all of these heart ailments is a better diet. We cover that all the time, whether it's different hospital programs that give people vegetables so that they eat better, or whether we talk about food deserts.

We are doing an edition about the (2024) Democratic Convention. The intern I have is working on that issue, and he's doing a great job. He's interviewing vendors about their issues with the city. The vendors are upset about the excitement about housing the migrants because it is more excitement than anybody's given about housing for homeless people. It's a very difficult thing because I'm trying to lay it out there as objectively as I can.

When I covered the migrant situation in November, I was at a luncheon where the Deputy Mayor for Migrants spoke, and she said that migrant policy is being decided by the Governor of Texas, not nationally.

I'm trying to find more stories like that where I get the vendors to break down issues and tell me what I should cover in a simple way. Vendors will sometimes write stories. We had several stories where vendors wrote about their perspectives on Chicago. And there's SportsWise. That's a column where they talk about sports of the moment. They did a column about their favorite Olympics, which will be coming out right when the (2024) Paris Olympics starts.

I also have a theory that newspapers shouldn't be all meat and potatoes. News is meat and potatoes. Sometimes you need salad, and sometimes you need dessert. And sports is dessert, sorry. I need to promote that a little more. That would bring in more guy readership.

I have a story coming up about a woman I interviewed 14 years ago. She had been a prostitute, and she started writing a book. She had little pieces of paper. Every time she had an idea, she put them into a bag. Now she has her own business as a contractor for the Obama Center and is producing a play about her life based on the book.

I counsel vendors to do the same thing when they're writing their memoirs.

The greatest way that people can contribute to StreetWise is by buying the magazine. We want people to buy the magazine and read it. People will say to me, "Oh, I gave the vendor money, but I didn't take the magazine." I don't want the vendors to get pity. I want them to get respect. The vendors, if they can sell StreetWise, they can sell anything. They can move on to something else. They can have a business, etc.

I don't want them to just be pitied and take money, and people say, "Oh, isn't that special? Isn't that sweet?" That's patronizing for all of us. I want them to take the magazine, read the magazine, and consider the things that StreetWise is talking about, which are marginalized people and the question "How do we make Chicago better?"

Everyone Needs Love

Pete
Philanthropist, Former Chairman of the Board

I'd seen vendors on the streets and interacted with them when I was walking around Chicago. I lived in the city for 15 years. But the first time I became intimately aware of how the StreetWise system worked was on April 29th of 2008.

I met a homeless man on a freezing, rainy day in April 2008. I was in my big, beautiful Mercedes right there on the curb, and 15 feet away was a gentleman who was in a kind of raggedy suit and tie. It was 6:45 in the morning, and this guy was sitting on the street, just trying to do the best he could to find shelter from the freezing rain.

I was like, "This doesn't seem right." So, I went out and said, "Hey man, you want to get in my car and warm up? These aren't conditions for anyone to be outside." And the next 45 minutes changed the course of my life. I found out his name was Troy McCullough, and he was a StreetWise vendor.

What I found out is that sometimes homelessness is not some permutation of mental illness or addiction. Troy was just damn unlucky. He was sober. He was a deacon in this church, but he had some health issues. He had a stroke, diabetes, lost his wife. It was a whole mess of a situation. He had been homeless for seven years before I met him.

I got to know him and helped get him in a house and get him a job, in addition to StreetWise. But he was a StreetWise veteran. I raised a bunch of money and started a website called SaveTroy.com. This is before Facebook. I sent an email out to my friends and said, "Help me save this guy. Help me get him a warm place to stay." And we did. We raised the money, like, overnight. We got him an apartment and helped resurrect his life.

Troy's location was in the corner of Michigan and Oak. Pretty high-profile location. Right next to the Four Seasons, which is where a lot of rich and famous people stay when they come to Chicago. Troy camped out right next to the Four Seasons, and he had a big personality, some interesting one-liners, and a big voice. He had these famous chants, "Read my, read my, read my, StreetWise, StreetWise, StreetWise." He was an entertainer.

There have been news articles written about this, especially in the Chicago Sun-Times. There's been CBS news stories on this as well. Let's see. *Formerly homeless man dies in his home. That was Chicago-born Pete Kadens who invited him to warm up in his car. He said he never could stand to see the homeless man suffer.* So, there are articles about it, but it's going on 18 years ago now.

When StreetWise found out about this, at the time, the organization was basically bankrupt. They were struggling. They were going to go out of business. They were like, "This is our savior. This guy who met one of our vendors and can raise a bunch of money overnight." I joined the board, and the rest is history.

There already was a board, but it was only about five people when I joined in '08. It was not a very fundraising-oriented board. I decided to go out and recruit friends and people with diverse experiences and backgrounds who could raise money or add money. I was like, "This Chicago iconic institution that helps hundreds of families is going to go under. We can't allow for that." I sort of leveraged my network.

The first guy I brought in was John Reinsdorf, whose family owns the Bulls and the White Sox. He really helped me, and we started building from there. A year or two later, one day we woke up and had 30 people on the board, and a real Executive Director or CEO, and the whole organization changed from there on out.

I served as the Chairman of the Board for ten-plus years and was heavily involved in resurrecting the organization. Do you understand the StreetWise model? Vendors pay $1.15, and then they retail it for $3. So, it's not a handout. StreetWise gives them access to some free meals and therapeutic resources, trauma prevention resources, but we don't do it for them. They have to want it for themselves. That's the difference between panhandling. Panhandling is you gotta have a cup, you gotta shake it. StreetWise, you gotta invest in yourself.

That's what the dignity of employment is about. The dignity of self-employment, the dignity of being an entrepreneur.

We're focused on bringing people in who have the will to get out of their situation, who want to have a roof over their head, and if they're willing to put in the work, we'll provide them the means to generate the income to do it. Then, we surround them with love. Everyone needs love, and everyone needs friends. The StreetWise community is a community of friends who support one another through good times and bad.

I remember the Thanksgiving meals with all the vendors. We brought everyone together. They brought their families, and despite their circumstances, everyone was happy. We did the best we could to serve food that was as good as you would get at a real Thanksgiving dinner. We served turkey and stuffing and jam. And man, those people had smiles on their faces. Those are the moments I remember, the interactions.

I spent a lot of time in the streets, you know, meeting panhandlers and trying to convert them to StreetWise. Explaining that there's a more legitimate way to make money. We have a system. You learn to be an entrepreneur. I remember those moments going out in the streets. I would usually go with a vendor. A well-known, prominent vendor would take me around and show me the different panhandlers. We would talk about converting them from panhandling to selling StreetWise. Some of those days were cold and nasty, but rewarding.

A lot of people, when they walk by a StreetWise vendor, think it's a form of panhandling. That people are lazy and are begging. No, these people invested in themselves. They are building this business, and they are maintaining their magazine inventory. The job of the board is to get the word out that this is a dignified entrepreneurial business model where these people have the will and determination to make their lives better, and so you should support it for that reason.

At the board meetings, we talk about the mission and ask if we are achieving the mission. The first mission of the board is to be an ambassador or sort of human billboard for what we do. The second objective is to raise money. The organization can't sustain itself without a million dollars a year, minimum. And the third is to offer support and help to the CEO. The CEO wants to help as many people as possible.

I have this thesis that the more generous I am, the wealthier I get. That's not about money. When I'm out there helping people who are on the verge of a crisis—I mean, not having a roof over your head, not having food on your table, it is a crisis, right—you're helping the most needy, the absolute most needy. That's God's work, man. That's important work.

It's easy to go volunteer for a nonprofit that's supporting a big theater or supporting cute puppy dogs. This is hard work, and it's not sexy. You've got to get to pain before you get to progress. Working in the homelessness space is a lot of pain before you get to progress. It's hard to lift people up who are in this space. If you can get that done, you can accomplish anything. Be generous. Be kind.

I would say in a weird way, I've gotten more out of StreetWise and the StreetWise vendors than they've gotten out of me.

I'm the largest donor in the history of the organization. I still say that. So, it's been such a credo for my life, truly. It's part of my legacy. Even though I'm not overly engaged anymore because I've moved on to other things, StreetWise is still a big part of my life legacy. And it wasn't just me; it was a team of people. I was the tip of the spear, but a lot of other people raised StreetWise up too.

(What I have to say) to the customers: Always pay your vendors full price. It's not enough to just give them a dollar. What that says is the service you're providing isn't of value. Like, if I go to McDonald's, and I buy a Big Mac, it's three bucks. You don't negotiate with the people behind the counter and say, "You know, Big Macs are worth two bucks to me; I'll pay two bucks."

It's a sign of respect. Vendors are putting themselves out there, and they're thinking, "I created something of value. I'm holding it in my hands, I'm selling you on it. I'm talking to you, I'm engaging you. I'm looking in your eye, and so if you value me, and you value my product, you'll pay the full price."

They're providing something of value that deserves to be paid for. They're looking for value exchange. If you can't give money, at least give a smile.

When you walk by a StreetWise vendor, signal to them that they matter, that they're important, that they're equal to you. Just by saying hello and smiling—even if you can't afford or don't want to buy a magazine at that particular moment—please give them the courtesy of saying, "We recognize you as a fixture in this city, and we appreciate you."

The Sense of Hope

Lonnie
Vendor

I learned about StreetWise through a young lady. At the time, I was on drugs and homeless, and I didn't know myself. She introduced me to StreetWise.

When I found StreetWise, I felt like I had a purpose. I got to selling magazines, and I worked hard at it. Money, everybody liked money, and it was all legal. It wasn't illegal. I got into StreetWise and just kept pushing.

I ended up working on myself. I met a good Samaritan, Pete Kadens. He approached me and said, "Lonnie, you've been selling a lot of magazines." He gave me a high level of confidence because he saw something in me that I didn't see in myself at the time.

I got married. I had some kids. I was thinking, "I want to be a good father. I want to be a good husband." I sold StreetWise for a long time. I made mistakes; I had a record. I couldn't get a job. I applied for good jobs, but it didn't happen.

I said, "Wow, StreetWise is all I have." So, Pete took a life into me and helped me get a job. Helped me with my family. This is a man that shared his resources with me, and I grew from that.

I've been a vendor for over 20-some years. Back in the 90s, StreetWise was booming. But now we're talking about the new era, the 21st century, and COVID-19 hit. StreetWise has changed. People have changed. StreetWise has always been an opportunity for a man or a woman, but it's harder now because of the new era. There are so many people facing trials and tribulations.

StreetWise gave me the chance to look at myself and the sense of hope. It gave me a chance to work on me. To see that I *am* somebody, and that I can make changes in my life. It motivated me to believe in myself.

It's a great opportunity to get out there and to talk to people, not only just to sell StreetWise. To let people know at the end of the day, you're not by yourself, and that it's going to be okay. But you have to keep going, and you have to keep working hard. You have to take it to another level, knowing that it's going to be a better day. Them better days outweigh a not-good day. I make the best of every day.

I realize that a lot of people are worse off than I am. So StreetWise gave me a whole different perspective.

Well, hey, you got opportunity with StreetWise because the job is flexible. You can do all kinds of things: you can be an entrepreneur, you can go to school, you can come back and sell magazines, and you can work on strengthening your education within yourself.

I enjoy being out there in the community and seeing so many walks of life. To show customers consistency and energy. Whether it's below zero or the weather is nice. You can come out and work with no cash, and when you leave, you have cash to get on the bus. Maybe get yourself something to eat.

People gotta understand that it's important to work instead of looking for a handout.

One thing I reflect on is time. Time is something you can't get back, but what you put into it is what you're going to get out of it.

We have younger people as well as older people that's at StreetWise. We always need more mentors at StreetWise because many people come in with hard emotions. We need more counselors to help them realize that this is life, and you are going to experience bad things in life, and it's important how you deal with it so you can move forward.

StreetWise made me very strong. It made me to know can't nothing stop me but me. It brings the best out of me. We are here on earth for a purpose, and you have to find that purpose. You have to look within. Always be grateful.

I remember when I got my first hundred-dollar bill. When a customer came to me and said, "I see you out here all the time. I appreciate what you do. Take this. You keep doing what you're doing. You keep working hard." That person gave me a hundred-dollar bill.

That just blew me away. I kept that hundred-dollar bill for a long time. It was a reminder not only of the generosity of people but that people look at what you do.

Still to this day, it's challenging. I have people that come up and say real cruel things to me. Instead of getting angry, I just say, "Thank you. Have a great day. I love you." Once this happened, and the person came back and apologized and then bought a magazine from me.

There's things gonna be said to you that's not pleasant. But when you know who you are and what you're standing for, you set a standard for future vendors. For anyone who's come behind you to sell StreetWise.

I try to give back to StreetWise. StreetWise means so much to me, and I'd like for these doors to stay open for people in need. I want people to be able to showcase their talents. I want to uplift them.

My advice for a StreetWise vendor is simple: Let me help you to help yourself. Let me just get you out.

I had dark times in my life growing up. So, take all your life experiences, the ups and the downs, put them in perspective, and do good. Smile. Keep going.

When I got off of drugs, I didn't know what I was doing. Trying to please people mostly. Going through the motions. Didn't know who I was. I had to find myself. What I did know was I had to keep going and do better. I had to work on myself. And I done that.

At StreetWise you see all the different walks of life or all the different characters who can play a part in helping you in life. They might need somebody to talk to. Somebody to show them love. Somebody to sit down with.

You could say, "Man, what if I was in their shoes? What would I do?" So, it's not easy. I don't have all the answers, but one thing I do know is I have love for people. I have respect for people.

Wonderfully Supportive

Saul
Vendor

Well, my mom used to buy StreetWise from vendors. That was how I first learned about StreetWise—because I lived with my parents in their house, and my mom bought the magazines. I became interested in vending StreetWise after I met my fiancée, and she had been homeless ever since she left her abusive boyfriend.

She tried to sell StreetWise herself, but she couldn't stand. It was too painful for her to stand for long periods because she had spinal injuries. So, because I was able-bodied and young, she thought that I would be better at selling StreetWise than her. Even though I worked part-time then, I didn't have enough money for a couple. I mean, we desperately needed extra money.

I knew StreetWise was a great way to make money if you couldn't support yourself. I wasn't homeless at the time myself, but I knew that I could easily become homeless if my dad didn't support me. My fiancée was homeless.

After I began selling StreetWise, I found it was a great way to talk to people. Because of my developmental disability, I had never had ordinary sorts of sales jobs that many people have. I found that I enjoyed selling magazines once I started. I'm sure you've heard from other people what a great source of cash StreetWise is. I knew it was the kind of job you could do if you couldn't support yourself otherwise or find regular employment.

I've been a regular vendor for almost 12 years now. I originally started selling in the early summer of 2010, but it was hard at first. At the start, I went back and forth between begging and selling magazines, but now I've been a regular vendor for almost 12 years.

StreetWise gives new vendors temporary IDs. When I first started, I would let my ID expire and have to get new ones, but then I wouldn't come back to buy new magazines. It took me a while to get into the discipline. There's a new issue mostly every week, and when I first started, I wouldn't sell out the new issue. So, I would keep selling the old ones which is against the rules. They used to have the rule that you needed to purchase 30 magazines. Now they let you purchase 20, and that makes it easier.

The StreetWise community is wonderfully supportive. I used to work in Wilmette, and there are fellow vendors in that area who have been helpful to me. The professional staff has also been wonderfully helpful to me, and none of them are snobby. They talk to us, and they interact with us like social equals. It's wonderful to be wanted.

The staff offers us a way to make money and support ourselves. Many of the people are here because they're homeless. Many, like me, come to StreetWise because they don't have any job skills. I couldn't support myself through regular employment.

I could say I'm here for the money, but that would sound crude. I really enjoy interacting with people. When I've applied to jobs that involve social interactions, they've told me that I wasn't qualified for obvious reasons. A lot of sales jobs are very stressful because the customers are nasty, but StreetWise is a low-stress sort of sales job that lets me interact with people who become regular customers. The people who buy StreetWise are pretty nice, so it's not like working in a retail job where the customers are frequently impatient, if not downright nasty.

Despite my experience vending, I'm still bad at social interaction. What I mean is I'm not a great conversationalist in the ways other vendors are. I don't promote a magazine like other vendors do. To be honest, a few people generally buy from me to support StreetWise, of course, but to speak bluntly, also out of pity.

To become an established vendor, we have to establish our own official location. In the beginning, I found that challenging. Other vendors would become angry with me when I would infringe on their territory, but I'd say that's a symptom of my own developmental disability and social backwardness.

StreetWise always made it easy for me to start again. I kept coming back to StreetWise and found a location in Wilmette. They told me at first that I should sell in Chicago, but I knew Wilmette and felt uncomfortable looking for locations in Chicago.

My fiancée said she didn't understand how vulnerable I was. My dad was willing to support me and provide me with housing. I didn't understand that I wasn't bourgeois myself. Just like my fiancée was, I was actually part of what Marx described as the lumpenproletariat, or as is known in the English language, the underclass. I used to think of myself as different from the homeless people I'd walk by. I realize now that I'm part of the underclass myself. I don't feel the sort of shame and insecurity in admitting this that I did when I was living in my dad's suburban house.

StreetWise has proved to be my most consistent source of employment and income. They provide social services here, and I've found them useful. They help me with my lease. They helped me stay on the list for Chicago housing. They've always been willing to talk with me about problems I've had in a supportive and non-punitive kind of way.

As you can see, I feel very secure. The StreetWise office provides you with a comfortable environment. I've made what could be described as work friendships. I don't socialize with any of the vendors outside the premises. But they have been willing to help me with other problems I've had. Here at the office, I can talk about my personal problems. It isn't the same sort of rigid distinction that there is in most other workspaces.

I have lunch at StreetWise. They provide free food here, which is a wonderful resource. Before they wouldn't let you take the food home, but now they do. It's been wonderful to have coffee, eat here, and take food home. But because of my own social backwardness, even though I eat lunch at StreetWise, I often do bring a bagged lunch. I don't spend lunch conversing with other vendors the way other people do. I usually just focus on my food. My fiancée found that very irritating when I would just focus on the food she had prepared for me rather than talking to her. But they don't seem to mind that the same way here.

I'm on disability, which would be barely enough to survive on, so StreetWise is a great source of extra income. Thanks to StreetWise, I've been able to maintain a bank account by depositing money from vending into checking and savings. A caregiver helped me establish a savings.

I have regular customers, some of whom know me from years in the neighborhood. There have been times when customers have brought coffee and food for me or invited me to sit down with them at the coffee shop where I sell magazines. StreetWise has provided me with a great source of income, social support, and a social network, both in the office here and with my customers in Wilmette.

There's one nice elderly lady from Wilmette who's invited me to sit down with her and her husband for coffee. There's another nice, elderly lady too. She isn't a customer. She doesn't buy magazines. But she wants me to accompany her across the street. I mean, so she says. She says she needs my help crossing the street. I don't think she really does. I think she's just being nice to me by making me feel like I'm helpful. Afterward, she always gives me money, which is charity, but she probably doesn't understand StreetWise. I'm very blessed that she's so nice and gives me such wonderful charity. She'll usually give me at least $20. I wouldn't have known her if I hadn't been selling magazines by the street she usually crosses.

There's also an old schoolmate. She was several years ahead of me at a special school I attended. She was in high school, and I was in elementary school. Now she sees me as a vendor with my own place, and she buys magazines from me. There are people in AA I know who buy magazines from me, too.

Because I sell in Wilmette, usually people are pretty respectful. When I tried selling in a couple of other suburbs, the police would tell me I couldn't sell magazines without a peddler's license.

It's challenging, too, if I'm in my spot and there's someone there from, say, the Salvation Army—well, this usually only happens around the holiday season—but sometimes there'll be people soliciting for Misericordia or Greenpeace or some other very reputable organization. I feel like I'm hugging into some of their profits. I generally try to find another location in those situations so passersby don't have a dilemma about whether to give money to Misericordia or to a StreetWise vendor.

Well, unlike a lot of StreetWise vendors, for most of my life my family took care of me. I'm mentally disabled, but my parents let me stay home instead of insisting that I live in a group home or care facility. I'm very lucky. I wouldn't be able to live independently now if my sister wasn't willing to co-sign on my lease. She's been very supportive of me. At least I am able to pay my rent now with the income I receive from disability, but I wouldn't have any extra income if not for StreetWise.

A Greater Empathy

Julie
Executive Director

My name is Julie Youngquist, and I am the Executive Director here at StreetWise. Everyone has different roles at StreetWise, but budgeting, fundraising, and all the accountabilities are on my desk.

I'm a social worker, and I've been in the field of human services for my entire career. I was formerly at a child welfare organization, so very different populations. There are kids from 0 to 21 involved in the Department of Children and Family Services, Juvenile Justice. That's a hard place to work for a long time. A recruiter on LinkedIn found my profile, reached out to me, and asked me if I'd be interested in applying for the StreetWise position.

I have been in the city for a long time, so I knew of StreetWise. I had a vendor in my neighborhood that I supported regularly. So, I went through the process, and on February 15th, 2015, I started as the Executive Director of StreetWise.

A misperception is that we're a homeless newspaper, and I don't even know what that means. What is a homeless newspaper? Another misperception is everyone who sells the magazine is homeless or has to be homeless in order to sell the magazine. That's not true.

Over the past nine years, I have seen changes. For example, I have seen the accelerated pace of digital over print. Everything is very much online. It's a cashless system. Even though our vendors are still very much on a cash economy, the people who support us and buy the magazine are moving away from a cash economy.

So that has been different. I think that today people are more aware of homelessness and the causes of homelessness. There's a greater understanding and a greater empathy for that situation compared with when I started.

Certainly, everyone experienced "life before pandemic" and "life after pandemic," right? Our experience with COVID and lockdown was unique. It opened up people's eyes to who the vendors are, what they're doing, and how precarious some of their situations can be.

On April 6th, 2020, we pulled the vendors off the streets. We had fundraising money for them. So, a lot of people got economic stimulus money from the government. Our vendors weren't eligible for that. But they came in here each week and got a set amount of money to help just offset their loss of income. We basically laid them all off.

People were all still coming into the office. Vendors were still coming in here, not just to collect cash, but we had to-go meals for them. We had hygiene kits. For a while, we were their only source of masks, hand sanitizer, and gloves.

We had just merged with the YWCA—Metropolitan Chicago, and they had a contract to do census outreach. That was 2020. They were supposed to do outreach with homeless people, and all of their partners were in lockdown, but we weren't. We were able to hire our vendors under that contract.

The vendors did that for about six weeks to get by, and we were able to pay them. Eventually, we went back to sales. So, we survived.

Okay, anyone who comes here to be a StreetWise vendor can be. The only thing that we ask of them is to complete an intake form. The main thing we need is their name and an emergency contact. All new vendors need to do the orientation. This is when they learn about what their rights and responsibilities are, where they're able to sell the magazine, and where they're not able to sell the magazine. We have a code of conduct, which is really just human decency, right? Be kind, polite, courteous, respectful, and consistent. We give them some sales tips, and then we give new vendors a temporary badge and 15 free magazines to get started.

They learn about our business model, which is the vendors purchase the publication for an amount less than what they're able to sell it for on the street. We are like a wholesaler. Vendors now buy the magazine from us for $1.15. They sell it for $3 plus tips.

People who are unhoused or unstably housed use StreetWise as their address so they can get government and banking documents. During March, there were like 20 vendors who got their voter registration cards here. It was so important to them to vote. They made sure they were registered, used our address, and then exercised their right to vote, which was awesome.

As far as my job, there's no such thing as a typical work week. There are sometimes 30 people here. Sometimes there are no people here. We're a human-facing organization, and we've got 130 vendors, and we know all of them. We know their situations. We've built relationships.

So, there are some days when you feel like you're at a wedding, and you go out and mingle with everybody and get caught up on what they're doing. But then there's running the business side of things. There are budget meetings, processing invoices, making sure we have cash on hand, processing Venmo, fundraising, talking with board members, and talking with people like you who are interested in learning more about StreetWise.

The most typical thing is that there's no typical week. That makes it interesting—sometimes very enjoyable, sometimes very difficult. But I love the mission, I love the organization, I love my co-workers, I love the advisory board, and I love the vendors. It's all worth it.

Many of the vendors who I've met here had a job and had a partner, and maybe the partner passed away, or the job was lost, and a new job couldn't be found fast enough. So, then rent couldn't be paid, and they were evicted. There are just these cycles that happen, and a lot of people are sort of one emergency away, or one paycheck away from experiencing that.

StreetWise has helped 16,000 people take a different opportunity to earn money in our almost 33 years of existence. Our StreetWise vendors have become part of the fabric of the city, and they're almost synonymous with Chicago.

A Communal Experience

A. Allen
Field Supervisor, Vendor

My name is Andrew, but I go by A. Allen. Before I came to StreetWise, I was into running because I had got sober. I got sober a year before I came to StreetWise, which would make me sober now 15 years, October 10th. I got into running, and I've completed three marathons.

Running is something that I like. Now I try to watch the marathon when it comes to Chicago. Oh, before that, I used to be a habitual criminal because I was a drug addict. I was a drug addict, and I was trying to get drugs by any means necessary.

I learned about StreetWise through a friend of mine from the neighborhood. He told me he worked downtown, and I thought that was exclusive to be working downtown from the far South Side, 109th Street. So, I asked him, "How do you get to work downtown?"

He said, "Man, I sell these papers downtown."

I asked him, "You think I can do that? You think you can hook me up?"

And he said, "Yeah." That was the beginning.

He brought me for the orientation, and I got 15 free papers. That's how I got started some 14 years ago.

I've had a lot of experience in life that was from the streets. I used to be...or try to be...a drug dealer, and I used to be homeless. When I came to StreetWise, I found people like myself. It's a community.

The StreetWise community is hardworking, honest people that's found a way up and out of the situation of being homeless, of panhandling, of being drug addicts. StreetWise, it's an honest way to survive.

The people that I get to work with are people like myself, okay? People that struggled in life and couldn't quite put it together, but nevertheless found a way up and out.

We believe in working where there's heavy foot traffic. This is how we make our money, you know, with the heavy foot traffic.

From the research that has been done with street papers, the most popular buyers are educated white women. To be in a position to sell the paper to educated white women, you have to be where they're at. Where they're at is either downtown or the North Side. People have had success on the South Side, but it's not like downtown and the North Side.

At StreetWise, our mantra is "A hand up, not a handout." This means we believe in earning our income. We sell the papers. We don't hold our hand out and ask people to help us out for nothing. We believe in working for ours. We have a button that says "This is my job." We work to earn an honest living.

StreetWise has shown me how to make an honest living and to be persistent and consistent. I go to my location every day at the same time and sell the paper and meet the same people. It puts some consistency in my life.

StreetWise helped me to have confidence in myself. That's very important because when I go out and sell papers, I don't have anybody from the office with me. I have to depend upon myself. If it's going to be, it's up to me.

StreetWise helped me with my self-esteem. StreetWise promoted me from a vendor to a field supervisor. Being a field supervisor, that's a position of leadership. I take more responsibility for other people than just myself. Responsibility and leadership.

StreetWise is a family among the group, and StreetWise is a family out there among the customers. I treat all my customers as if they're family. When I see them, they're happy to see me, and I'm happy to see them.

I used to write for StreetWise, and I used to get paid for it. They have invited me to speak to younger groups of people—like an intervention. To show the younger groups what ways not to go, because I've been there, done that. And if they take my advice, they don't need to go down that path.

To be in the office is a communal experience. We have little parties like Christmas parties and New Year parties. We've got an anniversary party. We've been around 32 years. At the Christmas parties, we have little gifts, and we have an All Vendors meeting. It's good to interact with all the people. Like I said, we're like a family here. And we're like families with our customers. At Christmas time, customers are very generous to us.

I have to mention this lady from when I first started. This lady came up to me and gave me $20 and said, "Keep the change," and took the paper. That was Monday. Then Tuesday, she came up and did the same thing. She said, "Here's 20. Keep the change." And she took the paper. Wednesday, she did the same. And Thursday. By Thursday, I said to myself, "This lady has been buying the same magazine all week." I thought she may have dementia. My mother had dementia. I said to myself, "Well, Friday, I'm going to tell her."

On Friday, I stopped her, right? She gave me $20, took the paper, and said, "Keep the change." So, I ran behind her, and I said, "Ma'am, I don't mean to bother you. But you bought this paper five times this week. You gave me $20 and told me to keep the change." She looked over her glasses...a little old lady...she looked over her glasses and said, "Young man, you think I don't know what I'm doing? Don't worry."

Proof

Daniel
Vendor

My name is Daniel. People tell me I look young. I was born in '85. I'm from Chicago, born and raised. South Side. Englewood. I'm 39. Now I'm at Roosevelt and Canal. I got my own apartment. I moved there fresh out of jail. Did 10. I had a lot of things going on, drugs, all types of stuff. When I got out of jail, I was 26. Right now, I'm trying to get my kids back. That's why I'm working.

StreetWise is like my own business. I've been a vendor of StreetWise for one year now. It's been cool. I get more than I would shaking a cup. I look down at people who ask for money, though I used to be like them guys myself. Now they see me doing something positive. A lot of them don't like that I don't do drugs no more. It's like night and day.

I want to tell readers about how I got to where I was. I know where I messed up. They say I'm bipolar and depressed. I'm not in that situation now. I'm not a guy who just talks about making a living, I prove what I do. My selling StreetWise is proof that I do good.

I got tired of begging. I wanted to buy my own food. I figured I'd get started getting back to work legally. I got work at a temp agency. The regular employees, though, didn't like that I got to be standing around. They had me picking up chicken off the floor. They drop some on the floor, and I pick it up. They at the temp agency knew what I could do. But the other employees, they didn't like me.

I have a forklift certification. I can drive a forklift, but StreetWise is my full-time job right now.

The challenges of being a StreetWise vendor is maybe getting robbed. Other than that, there really ain't no challenges. Well, the cold. And it get hot in the summertime. Other than that, as long as you nice, you get respect from other people. Everybody stop and talk to you. And they know me by name. Every day, somebody come and say, "Daniel, you cool? You need some food?" Yeah, every day.

Last year, the mail lady, she retired, came up and gave me 200 dollars. She said I'm doing better for myself.

StreetWise, they help me out a lot. My spot's Michigan and Monroe. People tell me I'm very professional. That's what the police told me. One police, he walk up and drop money on the ground for me to pick up, and he say, "I can't just give it to you. I want to say something to you. You carry yourself differently."

In front of the Gage last summertime, a guy took a lady's purse and coat. I was sitting outside the Gage, sitting there with my StreetWise. I stopped it (from happening). The lady ended up getting along alright. They feed me now at the Gage, but I don't ask for nothing.

I knew about StreetWise because I knew a StreetWise vendor. This was another guy in my same spot. The only reason he ain't there right now is cause he never signed up for that spot.

One time I got beaten up and robbed. After that, one guy gave me $300. That's right. When I was in the hospital, he sent $300 to me. He work in jewelry on Wabash. He give every five of us vendors in the Loop $20 for the same issue. So, he giving out like a hundred dollars a week. He work in the Jewelry Row and eat at the sushi place.

I have joys, but I get to them dark days. I see everybody walking with their kids. I want mine. My kids all the way out there by Gary. I used to cuss out the judge. When they took my kids, I was working, and I was in college. I was going to Ivy Tech.

One of my joys is I get to talk every day. A lot of people buy StreetWise every day, and people bring their dogs to me. Their dogs come running to me, and I pet them. But you go into Englewood, them dogs gonna bite you.

I deal with health issues like chronic illness. My doctors call me; they say, "Can you get your medicine?" The City of Chicago helped me. They gave me a big check because of my poor health. I like Chicago. I like going downtown even when I don't have no StreetWise to sell.

My whole goal is around my kids. The system say I gotta keep doing what I'm doing. I gotta stay positive. They had holiday parties at StreetWise. But for the holidays, I stay by myself. Since my kids been gone, that's how I want it.

A Blessing

Ruben
Vendor

I first learned about StreetWise when I moved here to Chicago. I'm from San Antonio, Texas. When I arrived here in Chicago, I didn't know the city. I saw a gentleman on Michigan Avenue holding a StreetWise magazine. So, I went up to him, and he introduced himself. He told me about StreetWise, and then I made the effort to come over here (to the office), and I got hired.

I'm going on a year and eight months. November will be two years exactly.

It's been a blessing because before I moved to Chicago, I did eight years in prison for DWI in San Antonio. I wanted to get away from my friends and my neighborhood, so I moved to Chicago. I was having trouble finding work. StreetWise gave me an opportunity, so that's why I'm committed and devoted to StreetWise. They believed in me, and God has blessed me, and everything is going okay now.

I remember the very first day that I got my 15 magazines. I was standing out there on the street, and I was telling myself, "I can't do this. I don't think I'm going to sell a magazine."

Then the first customer came up to me. She told me, "Good morning. I'll take a StreetWise magazine."

I didn't know what to do. I was brand new. So, I gave her the magazine, and she gave me $3. When I received those $3, that changed the whole thing. My confidence went up. I said, "I can do this. I can do this."

Then, about 30 minutes later, I sold another magazine. I just got to be more oriented, so I got it done. I got it done.

One thing I like about StreetWise is that I get to set my own hours. I get to pick the location downtown. It's a good way to learn the city and meet new people.

I like that I can work in the mornings, afternoons, or the late evenings. There's no dress code. You just need to treat the customers good and with respect.

There are some challenges that I face in the corner that I'm in. I get confronted, "What are you doing here? What's all this stuff you got here? What is StreetWise?" Just very threatening tone of questions, not just normal questions. They look at me like they want to fight. It's unwell people roaming the streets.

I'm on Madison and Wells. It's about five blocks away from the Sears Tower, so I'm right in the heart of the city. That's what I like. I love downtown. Being outside.

I love the entire staff. When we have questions, they listen and try to guide us. If it wasn't for the staff, it would be a little more difficult. The staff motivates you to get out there and do the best that you can.

I've made some good connections with the staff. I try to help the new people who are trying to become vendors. It's not for everybody. It's a little rough sometimes. Like the weather. I'm not used to this cold in Chicago. When it rains, you can't be out there in the rain.

I kind of stick to myself, but I try to be helpful by sharing my experiences and listening to people's stories. I try to be a careful person. I didn't make it for the Thanksgiving or the Christmas dinner, but I want to attend more StreetWise events. Everyone's invited.

Like I said, StreetWise has been a blessing, and it has impacted me in ways that I never would have imagined. I always look forward to getting the new magazines and being out there the next day with my customers. I always talk about StreetWise. Just grateful. Just very grateful.

I do photography and a lot of artwork. I sell my artwork and my photography work. Those are two of my top passions. At the age of 11, I started drawing. At about 13, I got into photography. I'm self-taught. I do a lot from fashion to street photography, to whatever catches my eye. From rainbows to spiders and little webs at the bus stop. From window washers at the very top of the buildings to down in the subways.

That's me. Being a StreetWise vendor and doing artwork and photography.

A Platform for People

Dave
Creative Director

I first learned about StreetWise in the early 2000s. I learned about it from visiting Chicago. I didn't live here yet. I was visiting Chicago frequently and became familiar with the street sales. I was a kid from Milwaukee, and at the start, I was too afraid to go up to the vendor and ask what was going on. I was at a Starbucks, and someone had left a StreetWise copy behind. I picked it up and read it. I was like, "Oh, this is what is going on."

I really had no clue. Like I said, just a naive kid from a different city. I wasn't connected to it. Then I had an "ah ha" moment. I realized, "Oh, this is actually real news." This is a very, very cool thing. I moved to Chicago in 2005, and I was working as a freelance designer. In 2014, some of my friends had started working at StreetWise, and they asked if I would consider coming on to design the magazine every week. I said, "Yeah, sounds fun." I'd already done a little bit of pro bono freelance work for StreetWise.

I started at StreetWise in November 2014. My first edition was the last week of December in 2014. By 2015, I had become the full-time designer. As the job progressed, I took on more responsibilities—not only its design and look, but content too. I also am a big part of all of our fundraising efforts, and I run our social media channels. At StreetWise, we are very much a family.

Working on StreetWise is fast-paced. We do a weekly magazine, so it's constant. We never really pause or break. It's constant deadlines. If I want to take a week off, I have to do two weeks' worth of work before I go.

It's important for us on the staff to be able to communicate openly. I'm glad that we can do so because a lot of the time we need to get resolutions on things right away. Because we're non-profit, we don't have a huge team behind us. Things just have to get done.

In 2020, we moved offices from Uptown to the South Loop, right next to Chinatown. It's amazing because we got these cool new offices. It feels very professional for the vendors who come in and want to purchase magazines, get some food, or meet with their friends.

I'm the Creative Director and also our only designer. I do all of our designs, anything from, of course, the magazine to designing our window clings. I design all of our emails, I design all of our social posts, I design all of our advertisements and everything we use to promote ourselves or our events. I have to step up to the plate when anything visual is needed. Through this job, I've even had to learn how to edit videos.

At StreetWise, we have a program that helps people who are looking for more traditional employment. Maybe they don't want to stand on the street with a magazine. We help people write resumes, get clothes, train them on job interviews, and stuff along those lines. We provide meals for people. They can stop in and eat for free so that when they're selling StreetWise, they don't have to worry about spending the money that they're earning on food.

We have a computer lab, so people can connect to the internet if they don't have any access to it themselves. We have annual events, like our fundraising gala, which is one of the main things that funds our organization. One of our biggest funders is "Give a Shi*t," which I'm wearing right now. With "Give A Shi*t," we have events throughout the year at festivals and pop-ups, and also at the website giveashirt.net. Artists donate designs every year. Their designs are printed on t-shirts, and we sell them at these pop-up events at festivals and online. 100% of the proceeds go to StreetWise. They've earned us over $700,000 over the years.

The objective of the organization is to help people get on their feet and find other means of employment. To become self-sufficient by being entrepreneurs. It all sounds very good on paper, but it's even better in person.

We have had the opportunity many, many, many times to watch people who are really down on their luck with personal issues raise themselves up. There are many ways you can get to the bottom of the barrel. I've been so happy to be able to watch people go out and start selling StreetWise to improve their lives.

When you're facing homelessness, it's easy for society to push people to the sidelines—making them feel unnecessary. With StreetWise, it provides a way for people to reintegrate into society a little bit. Now not only are they part of the community, standing at their corner, they're getting to know the people who are walking past—their regular customers, the people of their neighborhood.

Through that, there's so much self-esteem building. Vendors begin to recognize their self-worth and realize, "Hey, I don't have to remain on the sidelines. I can actually participate in society myself."

The self-worth identification happens to nearly everyone who comes in. Then it's up to them what they do with it. They can continue to sell StreetWise. They can work towards new futures for themselves if they want. We have our options once we're in a place to take that, right? We've had vendors that saved up to buy a car selling StreetWise. They sold StreetWise, bought a car with the money and now drive for Uber full-time. It takes a lot of dedication and hard work. It's awesome to watch the people who really stick with it.

When I see people getting back on their feet, discovering their resilience, discovering their self-worth, it's almost out of body. It's been 10 years, and I still get so happy when I see people change their lives.

For content, what we do is sit down as a group, which would be Julie, (Executive Director) Suzanne (Editor), myself, and Amanda (Director of Programs). We talk about things that are going on in Chicago, and we talk about our regular editions, such as the festival guide, which is our biggest edition of the year. We talk about things like farmers markets, communities, and we don't mind dipping our toes into some pop culture. When we do celebrity pieces, there's always a social justice angle to it. We don't talk about Taylor Swift's love life. We talk about Taylor Swift's philanthropic choices.

For the writing, we have Suzanne and me, and we have freelance writers and interns. Our vendors contribute to nearly every edition. We host a writers group on Thursdays. Vendors can come in, and they get to brainstorm topics for upcoming editions of the magazine. They get to write—whether it be a blurb, a quote, or a full-length article. They contribute to the magazine that way as well.

StreetWise helps a lot of Chicagoans get back on their feet. We literally provide a platform for people facing homelessness to express themselves.

We have helped over 350,000 people through the selling of StreetWise. A lot of those people have picked up, moved on, and started new lives again. Some of our vendors are offered jobs directly from their customers, so they don't even have to interview. Their customers will see them there every day and say, "I like your determination and how you're sticking with this."

Some of the vendors are paying their bills and living their lives, but some other vendors are really on the verge of homelessness or are already there. Our readers are often more affluent—maybe they have a little bit more wealth with some extra income that they want to share. Buying StreetWise is one way that they do that. The magazine speaks to people facing homelessness, but it also speaks to the middle class and above who are purchasing the magazine. So, we have to find that nice balance to connect the two communities. The key to that is informing people about things going on in Chicago and how it affects the different communities while they intersect.

StreetWise, especially when it first started, really made a huge impact. There wasn't anything like it. We're technically the third street paper in the U.S., and we're the oldest still-making. We've been uninterrupted since 1992.

During the pandemic, morally, we recognized that we can't be printing these magazines and then ask people to go out and interact with others and sell them. It was a very hard time, and we didn't know what was going to happen as far as our business. Our business is all based on personal relations.

But during the pandemic, other media outlets were covering how people who are facing homelessness are managing; this led to a lot of visibility. It led to a lot of donations that we then got to give out to vendors. We were able to pay vendors stipends while they couldn't work. It might not have been as much as if they were out there hustling themselves, but it was still something, and that was pretty amazing.

So, yeah, we're the longest-running without much of an interruption. And we're still going strong.

Read Up on It

Quanna
Writer

I grew up on the West Side of Chicago in the Austin neighborhood. I went to Lewis Grammar School. My grammar school was literally right across the street from my house, so it wasn't a problem with me walking to school. Then I went to Carl Schurz High School. That's up north in Irving Park in Chicago. After high school, I attended National Louis University, which was downtown. I didn't know what my major was. At first, I went with criminal justice. I hated it. So, I ended up graduating with my bachelor's degree in communications.

I first learned about StreetWise when I was very, very, very young. Me and my grandmother, we used to go to this restaurant at Hyde Park. It's called the Original Pancake House. I would always see this man in a wheelchair. He had no legs, and he would hold up this magazine, and it would say StreetWise. I always just walked past, whereas my grandmother would always—and when I say always, I mean always—stop, give a couple dollars and take a magazine.

I used to get frustrated at times because I'd be like, "Grandma, how do you know he's not trying to play you? How do you know those are his magazines?" And she's like, "No, I know that's StreetWise. Read up on it, read up on it."

One day we went to the restaurant, and I gave the guy a chance too. I bought a magazine, and I read it. I saw it was writing about all kinds of different people in different Chicago communities. So that's how I got to know about StreetWise.

Then, in college, we went on a field trip to the StreetWise offices. I'm like, "Whoa, this was in my life for a long time since I was a kid." I ended up writing an article that was published in StreetWise in 2019. The article was about how I grew to know StreetWise and what was my take on it.

I was overwhelmed when it was published. I was lit up. I was so happy with joy. I really couldn't believe it. I was like, people are actually walking on the street and purchasing the magazine with my writing and picture in it. I knew from there that I could do more.

I figure a lot of people don't understand the scope of how large the magazine is and how many people read it. All these people across many different backgrounds. When I was younger, I didn't think a lot of people read it. Then I started seeing a lot of people with this StreetWise magazine in their hands, so they're buzzing. That's also thanks to all the charismatic vendors. A lot of them put their whole effort into displaying how much this magazine means to them, and they like selling it.

I remember the field trip visit. At the time, they didn't have a big office. We were going into this building that had tons of files everywhere. They don't have a big global corporation. I remember them offering us food and showing us around the little small area that they work in, telling us all about StreetWise. It was mind-blowing to me.

My message to the vendors is to keep it alive and never let it die out. Like how my grandmother taught me about StreetWise. Keep it in the family, and spread the word.

A Different Kind of World

John
Field Supervisor, Vendor

I'm John, Field Supervisor for StreetWise. I learned about StreetWise back in the 1990s from WLS radio. They talked about StreetWise and selling magazines. At first, I got the impression that it was an organized panhandling, but then I learned it was entrepreneurial. At the time, I had two part-time jobs, so I didn't look into it.

In 2003, I went to Las Vegas for 10 years, working a full-time job at Healthcare Partners of Nevada. When I got laid off in 2013, I decided to come back here. There was more opportunity in Chicago, and I was familiar with the surroundings.

In Chicago, I basically had two choices: Work at a temp labor agency or work for StreetWise. I decided to give StreetWise a chance.

As long as you have a badge and current magazines, you get to pick your hours, and you get to wear what is comfortable for you. You don't have to wear some kind of uniform.

I started out as a vendor in 2014, and then later on that year, I was part of QAT (Quality Assurance Team) for StreetWise along with being a vendor. In January 2016, I became a field supervisor, which I've been ever since.

StreetWise is a community of people who care about one another. It's a different kind of world. You have a mixed bag of people. Some work a lot of hours, some have part-time jobs, and others supplement their income along with retirement, SSI (Supplementary Security Income), or another check. The extra pay may help cover their phone bill, their rent, or a vacation that they haven't taken in a while.

The people here are all nice in their own ways. Different opinions, different ways of living, and things of that nature. But when we come here to the office, our differences make us more like a family. A family that some vendors may not have ever had before, or may not have had in a while. StreetWise creates a family atmosphere.

The most popular areas to sell the magazine are downtown, Lincoln Square, and Lincoln Park. Andersonville is a popular choice, too. The suburb of Evanston loves StreetWise, and we've got a guy who helps supply food. He lives in the Skokie area. Those areas are very well populated with customers.

Also, the neighborhood North Center, south of Lincoln Square. There's other areas that have developed like Uptown, as well as Englewood on the South Side and Lawndale on the West Side. But it's not as well-populated as out there at Lincoln Square.

Another area that's pretty supportive is Hyde Park. There's a lot of good businesses down there. You have Starbucks Coffee. You have U of Chicago Medicine. Outside of those areas, other neighborhoods are kind of sparse.

There have been economic challenges over the past three-and-a-half to four years from COVID onward. We had a better opportunity before COVID than we do now, as far as recruiting new vendors.

I'm trying to be more in tune with what customers want. Back when I was at the Jewel Osco, customer service wasn't what it could be. It was a "customers are dime-a-dozen" mentality. If we worked at a retail store, as opposed to working for yourself selling StreetWise, a retail customer is not a dime-a-dozen. If you lose that customer, you might not get another one back. So, what you want to do is not take customers for granted.

Some of the passersby are respectful, but some say, "Oh, go get a job." Most of them say, "Oh, no thank you." Some of them don't even look at you. The biggest challenge is trying to get people who don't want to communicate to communicate. They don't understand that we pay for the magazines. The magazines aren't given to us. The vendors gotta save enough money to buy the magazines.

StreetWise gives out food and hygiene kits. Also, we have interns to help people if they need to get housing. We don't provide housing to people, but we can tell them where to go to get housing. Like on the North Side, 10 South Kedzie (Community Services Center), and a couple other places. But here at StreetWise, we're basically about selling the magazine and how to sell yourself.

StreetWise helped me make new friends. You don't have just customers; you have friends, too. I have a couple of decent friends sitting over there, here at the office. We're pretty friendly around here. When there is a disagreement, it doesn't become an argument. It's "agree to disagree."

I get opportunities to be involved in the magazine itself. We have a "SportsWise" column that we do—me and A. Allen, Russell, and William.

When groups come here (to the office), we make speeches about the StreetWise mission and story. Like when a group from DePaul or Loyola comes here. When we had more vendors, we would speak to more groups that come in.

Back when the Cubs won the World Series in 2016, I took a picture with a customer. A cool guy that works at Bank of America. This is Cubs Day, everyone's in a good mood, everyone's having fun. I made about $200 all in a couple hours.

But the main thing is, after the sales, we all go to the parade and watch the Cubs riding down Michigan Avenue. That was also the time when a group of us took a picture right outside the old StreetWise office on Broadway in Uptown, cheering on the Cubs.

The next year that same customer I took a picture with gave me two Cubs tickets and a hundred dollars in cash money for me to spend on it.

These are some of the big highlights for me from StreetWise.

Higher Powers

Dre
Vendor

I learned about StreetWise when they first came out. I was homeless. The magazine cost 25 cents for me, and then it sold for a dollar. It wasn't a magazine; it was a paper. I remember it was advertised on the news saying they come out with StreetWise to help homeless people have a sense of employment and keep from begging.

I became a vendor because I saw it as an opportunity to have employment. Let me tell you the truth about it. At first, I thought it was an easier way to get money so I could get drugs. This is in '94, something like that, when StreetWise first came out. I was an addict back then and a chronic alcoholic. I wanted an easy way to get money instead of just beg. And when StreetWise first came out, people was very generous with their donations.

But StreetWise, they helped me. They gave me resources. See, I don't do drugs no more. Right now, I'm in tune with my higher powers. I'm in AA.

StreetWise is a very resourceful place to be. StreetWise helped me pay my bills. It helped me get something to eat. It helped me to meet people. It helped me to feel good about myself. That's what StreetWise has given me.

StreetWise gave me clothes. They give me food. They give me companionship and friendship. They give me advice. They helping me find an apartment right now. Rashawn was teaching me motor skills on the computer.

They give me happiness, like when they have parties. Like on the 30th anniversary for StreetWise, that was sweet. It was packed in here. We had the back door open, the front door open. It was a beautiful thing.

I'm a veteran. Right now, I work for DoorDash. I'm about to get me some StreetWise today. It's working out cool. I make about a hundred a day.

So, I do my DoorDash, and I sell my magazine. One day I made more with StreetWise than I did with DoorDash.

The most thing I love about DoorDash and StreetWise is I can choose my own hours. Ain't nobody on my back. And StreetWise, if they have it, they will help you. Just like now, I'm here getting help for affordable housing because I got Section 8.

Okay, let me tell you this. I love my StreetWise staff, and they love me. They already know I'm gonna come in to laugh and join in. Especially Ron, when he sees me coming through the door, he's like, "Oh my Lord, who brought the cat in?" Julie would be like, "Hey, Dre, where you been? How you been doing?"

I told you, I've been here since they opened. I know everybody, and you know what? It hurts me when people leave. The staff, just like Rashawn, I came to see him today. He gone; he found another job.

I shift around sometimes. I sold StreetWise out on the West Side. I sold out on the South Side. I even sold in Bolingbrook. I'm not going to go to Humboldt Park because I don't speak Spanish.

What challenges? The weather and panhandlers are the main two challenges that I face. The rain don't help. The rain don't help at all. It's the rain that's the challenge, because if it's cold outside, I still sell. If it's snowing outside, I still sell. If it's sunny and hot outside, I still sell.

Selling StreetWise is a challenge in itself. It ain't got nothing to do with the neighborhood. Every neighborhood in the world got some prejudice in it. And me being 60 years old, I already know this. I have people used the n-word on me and tell me to get a job. Nah, ain't no different challenges in no neighborhood. Only challenge I have is when it takes me too long to sell my magazines. In any neighborhood, that's my only challenge.

One of my spots is Portillo's around 600 N. Orleans Street. If I establish that spot for, say six months, I got regular customers there. They see me, they're buying magazines, give me a fat tip and everything. But if I go there and there's another vendor there, I say, "Man, what's up?" That causes a problem because I done established that spot for six months straight. Literally working every day for six months at a certain time. But I don't fuss or fight about it. I got people there that I see every day. We more like friends.

One guy Venmo'd me $100. I never forget that. He bought the magazine and Venmo'd me $100. Oh, and this lady, she gave me $100.

She just came around the corner and gave me five 20s. There's a lot of people out here that have it like that.

Now I got me an apartment I had for two years. And, um, I'm a widower. My wife used to work here too. My wife died in 2011. We used to work at Portillo's because they got two doors. She'd be on one side; I'd be on the other side.

I'm getting closer to God as much as I can on a daily basis.

Thankful

Russell
Vendor

I learned about StreetWise by being out in the street. I had a part-time job, and I could see the guys out there selling StreetWise all the time. I could talk to them, support them, and ask about StreetWise. They said they lost their job and they're homeless, so they went to StreetWise.

A guy told me to come to StreetWise. I said, "Wow, I need some income." I got laid off my full-time job. I was there 15 years. I didn't know what to do, man. So, I went to StreetWise. And lo and behold, I started the same day. I got hired the same day and made money the same day. I never look back.

I've been a vendor for about 20 years. I've had my ups and downs, good times, bad times, but I like it. Some people think the magazine costs too much, or they don't come out on time. But the money, the money is good.

I enjoy getting up in the morning, going to my location, meeting my customers, greeting them with a smile or maybe a handshake. Even if I don't make that much money, I still enjoy selling my StreetWise. I look forward to seeing my customers, talking about sports, and asking how things are going. It's interesting. I like it.

The cold weather hurts sometimes. Sometimes it can be too cold out there to sell magazines, but I need the money, so I got to do what I got to do. I dress warm and try to do the best I can. I try to be there every day.

I sell my magazine down in the Loop area. That's the only place I go. I used to go for weekends, and I'd go to maybe a Catholic church on the North Side like maybe North Avenue and Wells. Anywhere that's busy, like CVS, Walgreens, or Jewel—somewhere I can make some extra money. I don't work on weekends no more. I just work in the Loop now, because it's Monday through Friday.

StreetWise has helped me a lot. They have AA meetings. They feed you. If you are cold, they take care of you. I'm very thankful. Without StreetWise, I don't know where I'd be at today. I was homeless for two years. So, I'm glad I found StreetWise.

I'm a nice guy, so I try to get along with everybody. Everybody's pretty cool, and they help me a lot. If I need somebody to talk to, they'll talk to me. Hey, look at today. It's Health Care Day. They took my blood pressure. I didn't even know I have high blood pressure. I learned that today at StreetWise. I'm walking around here, head spinning. I'm sick, but I now know why. It's because my blood pressure is high. So, I'm going to take care of that as soon as possible. Thank you, StreetWise.

When StreetWise has things going on, I try to be a part of it. The StreetWise Gala, I was there. I come to StreetWise some days, and they feed you lunch if you're hungry. They gave us tickets to the basketball games sometimes. Chicago Sky, maybe DePaul Blue Demons, or the Bulls game, the White Sox. I went to a baseball game last year, two of them. I saw the Chicago Sky win the championship.

StreetWise has very good entertainment. But sometimes you got to sit down and take it easy a little bit.

StreetWise taught me how to be disciplined. How to have respect for everybody. It builds my self-esteem up. I always be motivated to get out there and make my money. Even if I have a bad day, I'm still positive. They tell me how to save a little money. Put some money up for a hard time.

When they had that pandemic, I was messed up. I didn't have much money. I lost my job. I got a bank account now, so I save my money. I try to save something every day. If it happens again, then I'll be prepared this time.

I got some good customers out there. I got customers I haven't seen in a couple of years now. They still send me money through Venmo. A lot of people don't support StreetWise. They think I'm a panhandler. No, I'm not a panhandler. I'm a businessman. I buy these magazines, and I sell them. If I sell them, that makes me a businessman. Okay? So, this is my job.

At first, it was hard because people used to laugh at you all the time. "Ah, get you a real job and all this and that." It would make you mad, but I get over that. I just tell them, "This is my job."

I've been in Chicago all my life, except I was in the Marine Corps back in the 70s. I came back to Chicago, don't know why I didn't stay in the Marine Corps. I look back; I could have been retired by now. I'm 65 years old and still working. I'm selling StreetWise, so this is all I have to do right now. This is my income.

I sell my StreetWise so I pay my rent, buy some food, and have decent clothes to wear. Just to be happy. Always. That's the main goal. No matter what. Criticism, I can take it now. At first, I couldn't take it. Now somebody criticizes me, I say, "Okay, whatever, man. I'm doing my job, no matter what. It's not going to discourage me from what I'm doing. I love you all."

I want to say thanks to my customers. I appreciate everything you've done for us. Not just for me, but for the whole StreetWise community. We all love you all. Thank you.

Compassionate Hearts

MJ
Vendor

I became aware of StreetWise when I saw vendors on the street selling it. I looked a little bit more into it to see what it was about. They had a writing program. They were doing some kind of writing, and I like to write.

I had a need for a second job and the need for the money that the second job would generate. Things would be very dim financially without StreetWise. I would not have been able to keep myself afloat financially without it.

I've been a vendor for about a year and a half. I sell in Bucktown. Prior to that, I came in maybe 10, 15 years ago. I didn't stay that long. It was a short period of like 6 to 10 months.

StreetWise is a community that people are not accurately aware of. We are willing to sell a product that has already made a name for itself and to share information with the public. The news that's published in the magazine is very informative. The writing that you find in the StreetWise magazine you may not see in other places.

I enjoy a gamut of things about StreetWise. I like the camaraderie. I like when I come here to the office and see the office staff. I also like meeting the other vendors. When you come to the office, you get a chance to meet other vendors like you that are out, you know, selling. Whereas, on the street, I'm just going to my spot, and I don't have time to meet other vendors. So, I get a chance to meet them here.

I enjoy the fact that they do feed you. That's important because a lot of times I've come here hungry.

That's a plus that you can get a meal of quality. Also, I enjoy the customers that I meet. When I sell to my customers, I get a chance to meet the interesting people in the neighborhood. You know, I don't try to get to be their friend, but it's just nice to know them on the surface. I like to be able to thank them for supporting not just myself, but the magazine StreetWise.

I work another job. This is my second source of income, so because of that I haven't had a lot of free time to socialize. I wouldn't say that I have made friendships at the office because I have not been here that long. But what I can say is that I have great associations with the staff, and I've gotten to know a few of the vendors. I feel like I have a great working relationship with them as well.

Behind the scenes, StreetWise created this Venmo for us. That's a plus for vendors because without Venmo, there's a lot of money I would not have made. The other thing is that the staff talk to you when you come into the office. You can voice how you feel, or if you got something going on, they may give you some advice. They have meetings where you can sit and listen to what other vendors are dealing with. The staff can make suggestions about what can and can't be done.

There's quite a bit of challenges. Just trying to ensure that the spot that has been assigned to me is available because reclaiming my spot can be hard. Then on the streets, there's so many different facets of people that come by when you're out there. While you're standing there, they walk by as if they don't see you standing there. So that's like a whole big challenge as well.

Without StreetWise, things would be much more undoable. I wouldn't be able to achieve the goals that I have set for myself financially. There are times when I can work an entire day and maybe not make a large amount of money, but I still enjoy the spot I have where I'm at.

I don't get upset because I didn't make enough; I'm happy to be able to have the opportunity to try. You never know how the day is going to go when it comes to the compassionate hearts of individuals. Nonetheless, if I didn't have this magazine to sell, I wouldn't even have the opportunity to find out.

There's this little girl, and I'm not sure how she gotten to know me, but she comes looking for me. It makes me want to cry when I think about it. She comes with her dad, and she runs and flies over to me to give me $20, and I just be so blown away. I don't know how she got to know me, but she looks for me. Her dad says, "She looks for you every time."

I'm only in one place, but she just looks. She looks around to see if I'm over here. That touches my heart to know that someone that young would care enough to help on a consistent basis.

Then the other day, three little girls came running so fast, and they all gave me a dollar each. There's a lot of noise going on in the street, and they were coming so fast you could hear the noise of their running. That stole my heart.

I think it was yesterday, no, the day before—they came out of the store, and they wanted to give me the change they had. It was about eight dollars, and I was like, "Oh, my God. Did you ask your parents? Where's your parents?" I didn't want to take money from kids that hadn't got permission from their parents to do this.

They said, "Well, this is our money. My dad knows we're giving it to you."

I put it in a separate bag in case they needed to have it back, but they didn't. Kids value their money. It's just a little bit they have, and it was a lot to me. I felt kind of bad taking it, but not to take it made their faces look sad. I love the adults too, but it's the kids that steal my heart.

My experience selling the magazine has been enlightening. It has an array of things, like a spectrum of stuff. For instance, I have my little thing that I say when I'm selling StreetWise. I say, "We take Venmo." Sometimes you're talking and you don't know if people are hearing you or not hearing you. They don't look your way, and they just go on into the store or wherever they're going.

But then when they come back, sometimes they say, "You take Venmo?" So, you know they heard you. But there's so many of them that, for whatever reason can't afford to give or don't care to give, and you sometimes just stand out there losing hope. But then somebody donates, and it makes me feel like "Okay, maybe I'll stay and finish working today."

I'm experiencing hard circumstances at the moment. I just keep chipping away at it and working because I know that one day I will be delivered. But a lot of times I think "When?" Not so much "Why?" I do ask "Why?" sometimes, but then I say "Why not?" So, my biggest thing is that I just wanna get beyond my circumstances, so I can give back to the very neighborhood that has helped me.

I have passion and empathy and compassion to help people in a humanitarian way. I was blessed to be helped. This is my next stop:

I know most of the people from the neighborhood and can start my ministry there.

My ministry is something that gives to people on whatever level. If their car is going down the street and gets a flat, let me fix it. We'll fix it. I want to be able to do my ministry for the rest of my life, helping people.

This has always been my dream to have my own mission. I call it a mission ministry—to be able to help people do whatever they want to do. Somebody lost their bus card; okay, let me help them out. Why not? Because nobody else cares.

You've got to have an organization that cares, such as StreetWise. Because what is the purpose of life if we don't care to give?

Poem

***Roark
Vendor***

Choice

wisdom stands alone

like a silent partner til

fate is put to task!

Roark Moody (1950-2012)

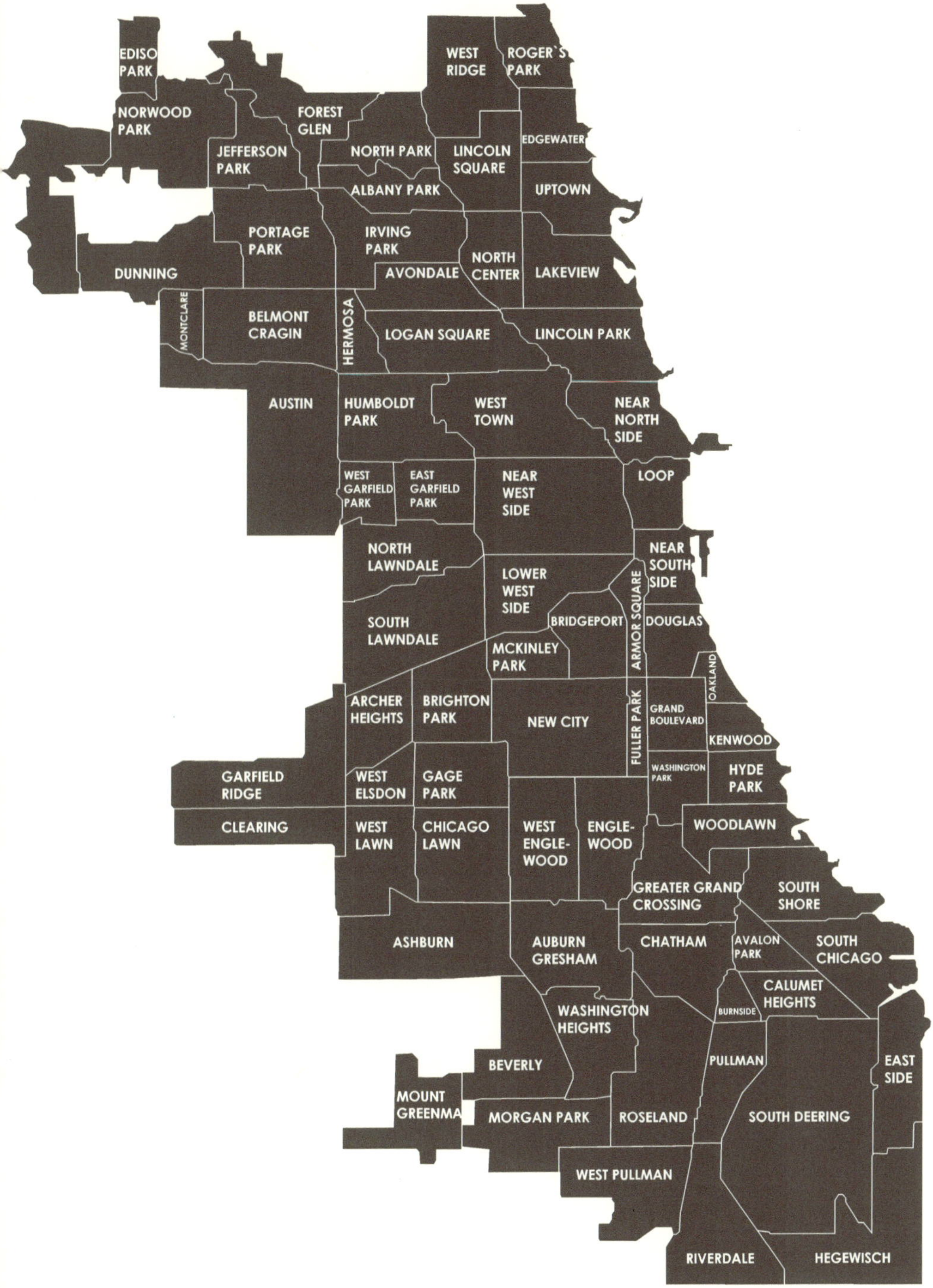
EDISO PARK
WEST RIDGE
ROGER`S PARK
NORWOOD PARK
FOREST GLEN
JEFFERSON PARK
NORTH PARK
LINCOLN SQUARE
EDGEWATER
ALBANY PARK
UPTOWN
PORTAGE PARK
IRVING PARK
NORTH CENTER
LAKEVIEW
DUNNING
AVONDALE
MONTCLARE
BELMONT CRAGIN
HERMOSA
LOGAN SQUARE
LINCOLN PARK
AUSTIN
HUMBOLDT PARK
WEST TOWN
NEAR NORTH SIDE
WEST GARFIELD PARK
EAST GARFIELD PARK
NEAR WEST SIDE
LOOP
NORTH LAWNDALE
LOWER WEST SIDE
NEAR SOUTH SIDE
ARMOR SQUARE
SOUTH LAWNDALE
BRIDGEPORT
DOUGLAS
MCKINLEY PARK
OAKLAND
ARCHER HEIGHTS
BRIGHTON PARK
NEW CITY
FULLER PARK
GRAND BOULEVARD
KENWOOD
GARFIELD RIDGE
WEST ELSDON
GAGE PARK
WASHINGTON PARK
HYDE PARK
CLEARING
WEST LAWN
CHICAGO LAWN
WEST ENGLE-WOOD
ENGLE-WOOD
WOODLAWN
GREATER GRAND CROSSING
SOUTH SHORE
ASHBURN
AUBURN GRESHAM
CHATHAM
AVALON PARK
SOUTH CHICAGO
CALUMET HEIGHTS
WASHINGTON HEIGHTS
BURNSIDE
BEVERLY
PULLMAN
EAST SIDE
MOUNT GREENMA
MORGAN PARK
ROSELAND
SOUTH DEERING
WEST PULLMAN
RIVERDALE
HEGEWISCH